INTERNET COMPANION FOR ABNORMAL PSYCHOLOGY

Cheryl J. Hamel, Ph.D.
Valencia Community College
&
David L. Ryan-Jones, Ph.D.

INTERNET COMPANION FOR ABNORMAL PSYCHOLOGY

Cheryl J. Hamel, Ph.D.
Valencia Community College
&
David L. Ryan-Jones, Ph.D.

As a user of this Longman textbook, we are pleased to offer you FREE access to our abnormal psychology web site, located at the following URL:

http://longman.awl.com/carson

In order to gain unlimited access to the site, please use the following password:

UPDATE10

Thank you for making Longman part of your learning process!

 LONGMAN

An imprint of Addison Wesley Longman, Inc.

New York • Reading, Massachusetts • Menlo Park, California • Harlow, England
Don Mills, Ontario • Sydney • Mexico City • Madrid • Amsterdam

TRADEMARK INFORMATION

Eudora is a trademark of QUALCOMM Corporation
Microsoft Internet Explorer is a trademark of Microsoft Corporation
Netscape is a registered trademark of Netscape Communications Corporation

The authors make no guarantee of any kind with regard to these programs or the documentation contained in this book. The authors shall not be liable for incidental or consequential damages in connection with, or arising out of, the furnishing of information provided in this book.

CONTENTS

PREFACE

The purpose of the *Internet Companion for Abnormal Psychology* is to help teachers, professionals, students, and consumers take advantage of numerous psychology resources on the Internet related to both medical (psychiatric) and psychological approaches to mental illness. The Internet is a world-wide computer network that brings computer users current information from around the world almost instantaneously, and the volume of information is so massive that a user must become savy about finding particular information. The *Internet Companion* will help you find particular information related to abnormal psychology by telling you about the types of information and discussion available on the Internet and some of the Web sites that are "master sites" for abnormal psychology. These master sites put together in one place an extensive array of links to resources both online and offline related to clinical psychology, psychiatry, psychological disorders and mental health. Many of these sites have organized psychology information according to topics frequently presented in an abnormal psychology textbook and so it is easy to supplement course textbook reading and get to precise information immediately. The *Internet Companion* is also a valuable tool for those who are looking for services and support provided by mental health clinics and self-help organizations.

Chapter 1 of this guide explains the Internet in simple terms. It includes discussion of the World Wide Web (Web), electronic mail (E-mail), mailing lists, and discussion groups. Chapter 2 presents helpful information on how to conduct research on the Web. "Surfing" the Web or using a search tool will lead you to a variety of types of information written by a variety of sources. These types of information are explained and the chapter ends with Internet resources for writing psychology papers. Chapters 3 through 5 discuss a variety of abnormal psychology topics and tell you how to find Web pages dedicated to these topics. In Chapter 6 you can find out about psychology and psychiatry as a profession. Several professional organizations with Web pages on the Internet provide lists of conferences, opportunities for continuing education, and current issues. The chapter will also point you to sites that act as an information service, providing information on current news and legislation related to the mental health field.

After these chapters you will find Appendix A which contains a glossary of frequently used terms. Finally, there is Appendix B which refers to major Internet sites containing large numbers of resources related to abnormal psychology. The locations of these sites are given in the Uniform Resources Locator (URL) format and a table for each site shows you the site's resources for mental health references, research, support services, and continuing education. The *Internet Companion* sometimes refers to Internet sites other than those listed in Appendix B. These sites will be accompanied by their URL address at the place they are mentioned in the text. Using your Web browser, you will be able to type these addresses in the "Location:" box and reach them almost immediately.

The guide does not cover all possible Web sites related to abnormal psychology that are available on the Internet. The references are meant to be starting points for further exploration of Internet resources. The guide can get you started by providing examples of sites that contain some of the information you are looking for, but there are many more sites out there than those to which we refer. If your attempts to reach a site are fruitless, as sometimes happens, try again later, just in case their server was down temporarily. Web sites often have an address change, usually to provide information more efficiently, and sometimes they go out of existence. If we have pointed you to a Web site and you receive a message indicating it is not there anymore, don't despair. Move on; there are plenty of interesting places to visit on the "information highway."

INTERNET COMPANION FOR ABNORMAL PSYCHOLOGY

Cheryl J. Hamel, Ph.D.
Valencia Community College
&
David L. Ryan-Jones, Ph.D.

CHAPTER 1
INTRODUCTION

We live in the "Information Age." All of us are aware that there is a vast amount of information available "out there" about any topic one can think of, including mental health and psychological disorders. Television, radio, and other media forms have brought the world of abnormal psychology into our homes and into our lives. In this new era of communication technology, the Internet (or the Net), with its vast stores of information, has become another important provider of information. The Internet is not as mysterious or difficult to use as it first seems to the novice; however, information available on the Net is growing at a staggering rate, requiring the user to become increasingly more knowledgeable about what it has to offer and how it functions. If searching on the Net becomes inefficient, users will quickly lose interest in this potentially valuable media form.

WHAT IS THE INTERNET?
The Internet can be viewed as a world-wide computer network linking a vast number of smaller networks together. The Internet is composed of several different kinds of computer networks, including commercial, educational, research, and government networks, each of which may be extensive or just local. Their computers contain large amounts of information, available for free in most cases, if you can get to the information via your computer. Each of these computers is uniquely named, and the type of network to which the computer belongs is identified in the last section of the name (e.g., .com or .co for commercial, .edu or .ac for educational, .org or .net for research, and .gov or .mil for government). This network of computers, once you and your computer become part of it, enables you to communicate with people around the world through a variety of methods.

Even a person lacking computer skills can take advantage of this exciting medium thanks to a distributed information system called the World Wide Web (WWW or Web). The Web gives Internet users a visually appealing interface to information in hypertext form that is called a *page*. *Hypertext* is simply a collection of documents that contain references to other items available to the user. This means that when a user views a Web page on the computer screen, there will be words that are highlighted and underlined, or there will be graphical icons that represent links to other objects on the Web. These objects may consist of things such as other Web pages, text, static graphics, movies, or sound clips on the same or a different computer. If your computer has the required hardware and software, you can begin to appreciate the Web's multimedia aspects.

WHAT ARE SOME OF THE INTERNET COMPONENTS?
Information on the Web can be accessed in a number of ways. To make locating objects on the Web easier, the *Uniform Resource Locator (URL)* format was developed. A URL consists of two strings of text separated by a colon. The first string specifies the method or protocol to be used to transfer the information to your computer, and the second string is the location of the information on the Web. When you select highlighted text or icons on a Web page, you are actually selecting the URL for the information that you want to find. The standard protocol for the Web is the *Hypertext Transfer Protocol (HTTP)*. The HTTP is used when Web pages are to be viewed across the Web. Web pages are written in a format known as *Hypertext Markup*

Language (HTML). The fact that the Web uses a standard transport protocol and a standard markup language allows any computer to access the Web regardless of its underlying architecture or operating system.

Another common transfer protocol is the *File Transfer Protocol (FTP)*. FTP was developed to allow Internet users to transport files across the Internet. Through a mechanism known as *anonymous FTP*, you can log on to a remote computer, locate publicly accessible information, and download the information to your computer without a password or system name.

Just as the Web is a distributed information retrieval system, there are two other retrieval systems still in use on the Internet. These are *Gopher* and the *Wide Area Information Server (WAIS)*. These distributed information systems were developed in the early days of the Internet to provide keyword-based search capabilities for users, but they have largely been superseded by the Web itself. This is because Web pages written in HTML are inherently structured to facilitate document searching by keyword. In addition, there are now many Web applications that have other search engines built into the software which effectively eliminate the need for Gopher or WAIS.

The Internet can be used to send messages to other users independent of the structure of the Web itself. The three most common systems for communicating with other users, depending on whether a user wants private, semi-private or public viewing of the message, are electronic mail (E-mail), mailing lists, and newsgroups. E-mail is relatively private, and in most circumstances, only the sender and recipient view the message. E-mail is not usually sent directly to another user's computer, but to a mail server to which the user can connect. Thus, messages may not be completely private. Both the sender and the recipient must have a mail account to access E-mail.

Mailing lists must be handled by a mailing list server such as *LISTSERV*, which is best thought of as a system to communicate with a restricted group of individuals who share a common interest (e.g., alcoholism, depression, or schizophrenia). Users of LISTSERV must subscribe to the mailing list of interest, and there may be very specific prerequisites for subscription.

The third system of communication is *USENET*, which is organized around several thousand newsgroups. USENET can be thought of as a discussion system which allows messages (or articles) to be posted and read by users of newsgroups with a specific interest in some topic (e.g., psychology, divorce, or hypnosis). Newsgroups serve a much larger audience than mailing lists because they are not limited to subscribers only. When you post a message to a newsgroup, your message is sent to several hundred or even thousands of systems all over the world who have a connection to the network news service.

The Internet is only one of the various networks carrying USENET traffic. USENET does not use HTTP to transfer news articles, but rather a protocol called *Network News Transport Protocol (NNTP)*. Just as E-mail access requires a mail server, network news access requires a news server.

E-MAIL
Electronic mail (E-mail) is fast mail service over computer networks. E-mail gives you the capability to send messages to anyone who has an E-mail address anywhere in the world, and they

will receive your message and maybe even reply in the same day! If you have a good E-mail program with a friendly user interface, it is easy to participate in this unique medium.

An E-mail program usually has several primary functions: to send mail and reply to messages in your mailbox, to save and delete messages you receive, to insert text files into your messages, and to write one E-mail message and send it to multiple sites. Of course, the functions are not limited to these, and as you learn your E-mail program you will gradually become aware of all of the options offered to you. The E-mail tool can usually be customized to meet a variety of your additional needs. If you have direct access to the Internet, you probably will want to use a program for E-mail such as *Eudora*. *Eudora* has all of the functions mentioned above and more, and is available over the Web from QUALCOMM, Inc. The URL address is:

http://www.eudora.com

NEWSGROUPS AND MAILING LISTS

Mailing lists and newsgroups have their origins in the academic community where scholars and researchers have used them to exchange ideas for years. With the widening of the Internet audience, more people than ever before may now obtain access to these scholarly discussions as well as other types of discussions of interest, giving everyone a great opportunity for broadening their education and keeping up with new ideas in the academic community and beyond. There are many mailing lists (many using *LISTSERV*) and newsgroups (most using *USENET*) specializing in various abnormal psychology topics that are available to the general public.

Electronic mailing lists operate by having electronic mail sent to a central computer, and from there, messages are posted by electronic mail to all mailboxes on the subscriber distribution list. To subscribe to a mailing list you need two addresses: the *LISTSERV* address for administrative business such as signing on, and the list address for sending messages to all the like-minded people who have subscribed to the mailing list.   Depending on the amount of activity, you may receive daily postings which sometimes create lively discussions.

There are several types of psychology mailing lists. Some psychology mailing lists have been created to allow researchers to exchange ideas and engage in collaborative work. Other mailing lists have been created to operate like "support groups." Many of these mailing lists are devoted to a particular psychological disorder, so that one afflicted with the disorder, or persons dealing with the disorder in some other way, can engage in discussions. When choosing which mailing lists to subscribe to, keep in mind that subscribing to only a few mailing lists could result in 50-100 messages filling your mailbox daily! Remember, too, that whatever you post to a list may be distributed to thousands of subscribers.

To subscribe to a mailing list usually requires only one E-mail message to the list moderator who will add your name to the list and send you directions for participating.

The reader or browser of articles in a newsgroup can step in at any time to browse the messages that are currently archived and then choose whether or not to reply. An advantage of newsgroups is that your mailbox doesn't fill up with messages coming from a list. But the disadvantage is that you are not notified of new articles arriving in a newsgroup, and so you must remember to check for new articles regularly.   Just as with mailing lists, there are newsgroups for every need, and many of the newsgroups have been connected with their counterpart mailing list so that messages to one are automatically forwarded to the other. In addition, many newsgroups have a moderator who screens inputs before they are posted to the group.

You should be aware that many, if not most newsgroups are not available to the average university, government, or business user. Individuals are not required to subscribe to a newsgroup, but their Internet provider must carry the newsgroup on its news server. Each USENET site makes its own decisions about the set of groups available to its users so you may have to request that your Internet service provider include a particular newsgroup in its available selections.

One newsgroup of interest to students of abnormal psychology is *sci.psychology.research.* Newsgroup names have several descriptive components divided by periods. The components become more specific as you read from left to right. You can derive from this newsgroup's name that it includes the scientific psychology community and that issues are research-related. Upon reading the group's charter you will find that discussions center around topics such as applied psychological techniques, current theoretical work, reviews of current journal articles, and grant searches. It is moderated to screen out non-psychology articles, personal attacks, political debate, and inappropriate topics such as issues related to individuals seeking help on a specific psychological disorder. To find out the purpose of the group and submission guidelines, access the *Charter of sci.psychology.research* at the following URL address:

http://www.coil.com/~grohol/psychart.htm

Most of the major psychology sites have links to several mailing lists and newsgroups related to mental health, therapy, and psychological disorders and usually will have the necessary information on membership constraints and how to join. By far the best place for getting a complete listing is *Psych Central,* which will link you to every known mailing list and newsgroup in the mental health and self-help areas. The lists are divided into two categories: "general support" and "professional." The professional lists are designed for individuals doing research or clinical work and carry prerequisites for joining. The other category is for the general public.

The *Western Psychiatric Institute and Clinic Library* site has information about mailing lists on psychiatry and psychology. There you will be able to read a short description of each mailing list and learn the address of the list administrator if you care to join. Although most of the mailing lists they refer to are for professionals, sometimes students are allowed to join. The site also has a listing entitled "Psychiatric and Psychological USENET Groups." The groups are divided into "alt." groups which present an alternative point of view, "sci." groups which specialize in scientific research and applications, and "soc." groups which look at social issues and world cultures.

Many mailing lists and newsgroups will give you information about participation after you join. If not, it is wise for a novice to start by listening and observing before posting any messages to find out the particular conventions of a group. A quick way to find out the knowledge level or restrictions of the group is to check the FAQ file or a summary of past discussion topics, if these have been archived and are available. Then, use care in composing messages so that they are clear expressions of your ideas and are courteous. In addition, take the time to decide whether it would be more appropriate to send your message to the entire group or to respond to only one person via his or her E-mail address. Responses to individuals cut down on message traffic and may often be the better choice.

GETTING CONNECTED

None of the features of the Internet can be accessed without the appropriate software for your computer. The Web is best accessed with a Web browsing program. Although there are many browsers available, the two most widely used browsers are *Microsoft Internet Explorer* and *Netscape Navigator*. More recent versions of these browsers have more capabilities than earlier versions and so you can do more with them. For example, you can print from the screen with *Netscape Navigator 3.0*, but can't with version *1.0*. Even the most up-to-date browsers do not include all of the software that you will need to take advantage of all of the components of the Internet or to access all of the information on the Internet, but usually the browser allows the supporting software to be identified and called from the browser itself.

Internet Explorer is free from Microsoft and is currently in version *3.0* with a *4.0* in beta test. *Internet Explorer 4.0* is an integrated package with more than just a browser. The Microsoft Internet site is located at the following URL address:

http://www.microsoft.com

Netscape Navigator must be purchased. Netscape also has a new integrated package called *Communicator*. To reach their Net site go to the following URL address:

http://www.netscape.com

You must also get Net access through an Internet service provider, a company that has the computers and leased lines to act as your gateway to the Internet. *America Online* and *CompuServe* provide Internet access, among other online services. There are several providers who provide Internet access only. Either way, you pay a monthly fee to "dial in" to access the online services.

While the Web at first glance seems very complex and potentially difficult to use, the best approach is to get on the Web and become familiar with it. It is both fun and educational.

CHAPTER 2
CONDUCTING RESEARCH ON THE INTERNET

The Internet can bring you the latest research and discussion on "hot" topics in abnormal psychology. Information on the Internet is less than a year old, in most cases, and updates are frequent. The Net gives you a window to "living" psychology where you quickly gain a sense of how practitioners and researchers around the world live and breathe psychology in their daily lives. In that sense, the Internet is not like a college library, full of the history and traditions of psychology. Instead, you get the psychology of the "here and now." A keyword search on the Internet is very likely to lead you to an article in a recently published psychology newsletter, or a list of the current research projects at a renowned research institute. Searches often lead to another important source of information on the Internet--the popular *USENET* newsgroups on a large variety of psychology-related subjects. Here you will find discussions of current issues in psychology as viewed by academics and practitioners, or you can become part of a support group for the general public. Mailing lists and newsgroups were discussed in detail in Chapter 1.

Information on the Internet is distributed from a variety of sources in a variety of styles. There are mental health articles, designed to be "brochures" for the general public. Other sites present information using the FAQ (Frequently Asked Questions) format, again usually for the general public. There are research articles, book reviews, news, and abstracts (short summaries of articles) designed for professionals. In order to better evaluate the information you receive, you need to know something about the purpose and sources of these various types of information.

In the past, the Internet centered around the exchange of science and research information. Use of the Internet for commercial purposes, such as product advertising, was frowned upon. Today, the basic infrastructure of the "network of networks" is changing hands--from government and education networks to commercial and special interest networks. With the commercialization of the Internet, the number of Web sites are growing at a staggering rate, and it now takes longer to find scholarly and scientific information. To save time and make your travels on the "information highway" more efficient, Appendix B presents a number of "master" sites for abnormal psychology. These sites were so named because they have extensive amounts of information concerning mental health, psychological disorders, research, support services, and continuing education in the field of abnormal psychology, so much information that you will want to bookmark these sources so that you can return to them again and again. Some of the master sites come from educational institutions and the informational resources are of an academic nature; other sites are brought to you as commercial services and so tend to have free services as well as services to sell. Some of the sites will inform you of their intended audience, for example, consumers, professionals, students, the world. The remainder of this chapter shows you the types of information available through these sites. If you do not find the information you are seeking by using the "master" sites then it is suggested that you use one of the many search tools available through your Web browser.

Since the Internet is largely unregulated, remember to always evaluate your findings by considering the source of the information. Remember, too, that just because there is a Web site doesn't mean the information at that site is correct!

MENTAL HEALTH ARTICLES

The Internet has an outstanding potential to disseminate mental health information to large audiences, and so you see a wealth of what might be called mental health "fact sheets" on the Net. These are brochure-like information presentations on various mental health topics such as schizophrenia, depression, anxiety disorders, etc. Most are published by reputable national organizations, such as the American Academy of Child and Adolescent Psychiatry (AACAP) or the American Psychological Association (APA). For instance, the AACAP publishes online *Facts for Families (FFF)* brochures to educate parents and families about psychiatric disorders affecting children and adolescents. The URL address for the AACAP is:

http://www.aacap.org/web/aacap/

A representative master site containing this type of mental health information is *Online Psych*. Their alphabetized list of topics contains more than 250 Internet links in 25 different areas related to psychological conditions and mental health services available to the general public. Many of the links are to the type of articles we have described here, where the article content is written in layman's terms. Computer users are also provided links to mailing lists and newsgroups related to the topic.

There is also much scholarly information on the Internet intended for the academic community and professionals in the field. The scholarly information is likely to be located in electronic journals or presented by academic institutions. *Psych Web*'s "Scholarly Psychology Resources on the Web" and *Clinical Psychology Resources* have hundreds of such references sorted by topic. Of course, most of academic psychology remains offline rather than on the Internet itself, but online access to library catalogs and indices to databases are invaluable for helping you find what you want. Most of the master sites in Appendix B provide links to bookstores and book publishers as well, and several of the sites give you lists of psychology books, magazines, and journals to help you get to information in print form. Several of the master sites offer opportunities for ongoing scholarly discussion of important topics in mental health through a "discussion forum" that can be entered into at any time.

WHAT ARE FAQs?

Another format for the presentation of mental health information is the Frequently Asked Questions (FAQ) page. As you might guess, these pages present in-depth information on a particular mental health topic in a question-and-answer format. Designed for the general public, the FAQs are presented in layman's terms. The APA's *PsychNET*, *Online Psych*, *Internet Mental Health Resources*, *Psych-Link*, and *Psych Web* have numerous links to information of this sort. Most of the USENET newsgroups have FAQ files that give you a wealth of information about their newsgroup's focus. You can access a Web page with links to all the USENET newsgroup FAQ files by typing the following URL address:

http://www.cis.ohio-state.edu/hypertext/faq/usenet/FAQ-List.html

ELECTRONIC JOURNALS

The term "electronic journal" is seen frequently as one browses the Web sites related to psychology, but there is little consistency in how the term is being used. In a conservative sense, electronic journals are viewed as electronic versions of the "paper" journals archived in our public libraries. But in many ways this is a narrow view when one considers the multimedia opportunities the Internet provides. A more visionary view of electronic publishing includes presentation of visual and auditory information, easy archiving of past issues, searchable indices, hyperlinks to related information, and fast peer feedback, and these are only a few of the advantages of this type of publishing.

Behavioral and Brain Sciences Target Article Preprints is an electronic journal published by Cambridge University Press. The journal contains controversial articles in biology, cognitive science, artificial intelligence, linguistics, and philosophy. Articles are reviewed by peers and commentaries are invited. The commentaries, the target article, and the author's responses are then published simultaneously. You can view the journal's contents by accessing the following URL address:

http://www.princeton.edu/~harnad/bbs/

ECT On-Line is an electronic journal from Great Britain open to writing and discussion on the topic of electroshock therapy. The journal contains instructions for submission of articles, which are peer-reviewed, and presents abstracts of all articles accepted for online publication. You can reach the site of this journal at the following URL address:

http://www.priory.co.uk/journals/psych/ectol.htm

Psycoloquy is an electronic journal sponsored by the APA and it has a format similar to the journals already described. The journal publishes refereed articles and peer commentary. You can reach this journal through the following URL address:

http://www.princeton.edu/~harnad/psyc.html

Psychiatry On-Line, is an international journal available purely on the Web and it is free. Just like "paper" journals, all articles are reviewed by peers before being published and articles from previous issues are archived (electronically). You can visit this site at the following URL address:

http://www.priory.com/journals/psych.htm

For a very comprehensive list of electronic journals that publish full online articles, use mulitmedia formats, or have peer commentaries, visit the *Clinical Psychology Resources* site or *Psych Web*.

Most psychology journals in paper form can be found on the Internet, but the journals vary tremendously in the amount of information that they publish online. Some provide only a table of contents of each issue, while others provide abstracts only. In these cases, an actual article must be obtained from the "paper" journal. Only a few publish complete articles online, and then the numbers vary from one article per issue, a few selected articles, or the entire issue. If you ever need quick access to a good list of psychology journals, the abnormal psychology master sites in Appendix B provide several. The lists of journals have been created so that if you click on a name of a journal on the list you will get subscription information, but many of the lists will also give you online access to the journals' tables of contents and/or abstracts of articles. If the journal puts self-contained articles on the Web, it will be possible to access the article immediately. *PsycSite* has links to two very comprehensive journal lists, one published by Guenther and the other by Krantz. Using Guenther's list of almost 1,000 links to psychology and social science journal sites, you can use a search tool to go directly to journals in a category (e.g. clinical psychology) and from there you can view all the listed journals or narrow your list to only those containing full-text articles. Using Krantz's list, you can search psychology-related journals listed in alphabetical order by journal name and find out immediately whether you can access a table of contents, subscription information only, abstracts, and/or full-text articles.

LIBRARY CATALOGS

One way to find information on a given topic is to go to a library and use its catalog. The Internet gives you the opportunity to search several library catalogs while sitting at your computer. If the catalog search results in an article or book that you are interested in, you usually can get it through interlibrary loan. *Cyber-Psych* has a good list of library catalogs that allow online access to the general public.

The *Library of Congress Information System* offers Web-based Z39.50 client interfaces to over 90 online library catalogs and databases inside and outside the Library of Congress. You can reach this service at the following URL address:

http://lcweb.loc.gov/homepage/online.html

Many state government libraries and state university libraries also offer Z39.50 search tools.

DATABASES AND ARCHIVES

A frequently searched database pertaining to education research is the Educational Research Information Clearinghouse (ERIC). You can search this database using *AskERIC* to find useful reports and then request copies which are provided for a fee. To use *AskERIC* go to the following URL address:

http://ericir.syr.edu/

Very large databases containing abstracts of articles from psychology-related journals are maintained by the APA. It is not possible to access these databases without paying a subscription fee and the cost is prohibitive for individuals. You can find out more about these electronic databases by accessing *PsychInfo* through the APA's *PsychNET* home page. Recently, the APA has created at its Web site a new search engine called *PsychCrawler* that can search the APA and National Institute of Mental Health (NIMH) Web sites only. You will get information in various forms, sometimes just a title and reference, and other times a full article, such as a book review.

The Counseling in Primary Care Trust in Great Britain has created a free search service called *Counsel.Lit*. You can search a database of almost 2,000 entries, including journal articles, reviews, and research abstracts related to counseling in primary care. Their URL address is:

http://psyctc.sghms.ac.uk/cpct/counsellit1.htm

CyberPsych provides links to archives of scholarly articles on specific topics in psychology, such as the Alcoholism Research Database. The *Clinical Psychology Resources* Web site from Germany has a large database of full-text articles related to clinical and health psychology that have been published online from around the world.

Guenther, at the University of Augsburg, Germany, has created a search tool called *Psycharticle Search* which can search for full articles in APA journals, the MEDLINE database and other databases. You can access this search tool at the following URL address:

http://www.wiso.uni-augsburg.de/sozio/hartmann/psycho/jsearch.html

For anyone interested in medical or psychiatric information, archives from the American Medical Association journals can be searched through the *AMA-Journal Search Form* located at the following URL address:

http://www.ama-assn.org/cgi-bin/search

Internet resources related to psychiatry and abnormal psychology can be found by using a service of the National Library of Medicine (NLM) to search 9 million citations in the Medline database. You will get a short abstract of a published article and the reference information to find it in a library. The URL address for this search service is:

http://www4.ncbi.nlm.nih.gov/PubMed

SEARCH TOOLS

It is possible to search directly for information on a particular topic in psychology by using a search tool, or "search engine," as they are sometimes called. A typical Web-based search tool lets you type in a keyword and the program immediately conduct a search of the Web.

If you are using an advanced Web browser, like *Netscape Navigator 3.0*, you will be able to click on an icon which will provide you with several search tools to choose from. One of the most powerful search tools is *AltaVista*, which uses a very powerful query language to search Web sites and *USENET* newsgroups. The various search engines are designed differently. *Excite* searches 50 million Web pages, about 140,000 Web site listings, and thousands of *USENET* postings. With the added use of Intelligent Concept Extraction (ICE), which relates your key word to other words on the Web that are similar in concept, you are likely to get an unwieldy large number of "hits." *WebCrawler*, on the other hand, searches an index that is updated daily. The index is based on page titles and URL contents only, which means you get fewer "hits," but they are likely to be very close to what you are looking for. *Yahoo* has a very extensive hierarchical topic index which may lead you to relevant "hits" quickly.

As with any search function, very specific keywords may result in no findings. If this happens, use a more general keyword to increase your chances of finding related information. Each search tool has information on how to use the query language to get the best results. This information is usually in the Help section.

These search engines can be accessed directly through their URL addresses, which are listed below:

http://www.altavista.digital.com
http://webcrawler.com.html
http://www.excite.com
http://www.yahoo.com

Most search services are free, but more may very soon become commercial and charge per query. With the ever increasing load on the free search servers, many users will gladly pay a service charge to save time when conducting searches.

SOFTWARE AND SHAREWARE
A variety of software to conduct experiments, present computer simulations, and analyze classroom data etc. can be obtained over the Web. Sometimes software (trialware) can be downloaded and used for a trial period absolutely free, giving you a chance to evaluate its usefulness. This software may sometimes be just a "demo," or may have some features that are disabled until you pay to use them (crippleware). Shareware is usually copyrighted and it is best to pay the requested fee to avoid potential problems in the future. Catalogs of software for psychology, which describe software packages and give purchase information, are available online through *PsycLink*. The URL address is:

http://www.plattsburgh.edu/psyclink

PsycSite has a list of resources that will point you to several sites where you can browse catalogs or download programs.

TIPS FOR WRITING PAPERS
PsycSite includes a "Student Centre" which provides pointers to sites of special relevance to psychology students. You will be directed to useful information about the *American Psychological Association Style Manual* and other advice for writing papers.

If you are writing a research report or term paper and are using Internet information, you will have to know about the current standards for referencing electronically published information. The American Psychological Association has provided examples of a variety of Web citations in acceptable APA style. You can access these examples at the following URL address:

http://www.apa.org/journals/webref.html

CHAPTER 3
WEB PERSPECTIVES ON ABNORMAL PSYCHOLOGY

The Internet began as a networking of a few major universities in the U.S. who used it to communicate scientific and academic information among themselves. With the introduction of the World Wide Web and other significant advances in Internet technology, the sharing of information is now a world-wide happening. If there is a computer anywhere in the world with information available it is now possible for any person to access it from anywhere in the world. In addition, documents can be created by inexperienced computer users so that these users can contribute to an ever-expanding database of documents on the Web. Internet users consist of computer technologists, academic communities, scientists, military and government institutions, commercial enterprises, and the general public. It is easy to understand why information about abnormal psychology on the Internet is brought to you from a variety of perspectives. The Internet brings you information about the field of abnormal psychology from, among others, historical perspectives, various theoretical perspectives, from medical perspectives, and from the perspectives of former mental patients.

HISTORY OF PSYCHOLOGY
Two good starting points to find information about the history of psychology, and the history of mental illness and treatment, are the master psychology Web sites *Psych Web* and *PsySite*. Both sites have a number of links to resources on these subjects and they are categorized under the heading, "History of Psychology."

A very good starting point for understanding the ideas from which psychology originated is a Web site called *Mind and Body: Rene Descartes to William James*. This site presents quite lengthy discussions about mind/body dualism, the rise of experimental psychology, and the beginnings of American psychology. The site includes excellent graphics. You can reach this Web page, a history of psychology timetable, historic milestones in neuroscience, and a short history of lobotomy from the *Resources in the History of Psychology* site at the following URL address:

http://198.49.179.4/pages/awalsh/psych-history.html

Another very good site for an historical perspective of the field of abnormal psychology is the *History of Psychology* page from Athabasca University in Alberta, Canada. Visit the site to find out more about Abraham Maslow, the "founder" of humanistic psychology, and information about other historical figures in psychology, visit the *History of Psychology* site. Their URL address is:

http://server.bmod.athabascau.ca/html/aupr/history.htm

Current articles related to the history of psychology can be obtained by reading the newsletter of the American Psychological Association (Division 26) History of Psychology. You can access the Division 26 newsletter and all online articles by going to the APA master site *PsychNet*. The Canadian Psychological Association (Section 25) History and Philosophy of Psychology publishes their bulletin on the Net. You can access all bulletin articles published online using the following URL address:

http://www.yorku.ca/dept/psych/orgs/cpa25/bulletin.htm

FREUD ARCHIVES
Articles related to the life and work of Sigmund Freud and links to many more sources of information can be obtained at the *A. Brill Library of the New York Psychoanalytic Institute.* Here you will also find news and discussions of contemporary ideas in psychoanalysis and links to the New York Psychoanalytic Institute and Society. Their URL address is:

http://plaza.interport.net/nypsan/

The *Alfred Adler Institute of San Francisco* Web site contains information about classical Adlerian psychology. There are a number of readings about the theory and practice of Adlerian psychology, several biographical sketches of Adler and his followers, and remembrances of other early contributors to psychology. To reach this Web site, go to the following URL address:

http://www.behavior.net/orgs/adler/index.html

Through *MedWeb* you can access several additional links to learn more about Freud, his daughter, and Freud contemporaries, such as Carl Jung. The URL address for *MedWeb*'s history page is:

http://www.gen.emory.edu/MEDWEB/keyword/history.html

What makes the Internet so interesting is that we can usually find many perspectives on any issue as we "surf" the Web. The topic of Freud is no different, and so we have *Burying Freud.* Here you will find extensive discussion and debate by academics, practitioners, and patients about the value of Freud's work and the validity of the psychoanalytic approach. Their URL address is:

http://www.shef.ac.uk/uni/projects/gpp/burying_freud.html

HUMANISM AND OTHER PERSPECTIVES
You will be able to reach several sites devoted to humanistic psychology by accessing *Psych Web*'s "Scholarly Psychology Resources."

Some information about George Kelly, one of the early personality theorists who promoted a constructivist system of psychology, can be found at the *Personal Construct Psychology* Web site. The site which, among other things, provides an historic overview of Kelly's work can be accessed at the following URL address:

http://ksi.cpsc.ucalgary.ca/PCP/PCP.html

An interesting full-text online article entitled, "On the History of Developing Behaviorism That You Won't Find in Most History of Psychology Textbooks" (book review) can be found at the following URL address:

http://www.apa.org/journals/cnt/jan97/allport.html

PSYCHIATRY ON THE WEB

Information about mental health and mental disorders from a psychiatric perspective is abundant on the Web. Most Web resources that discuss psychological disorders refer to the official diagnostic criteria used by psychiatrists, psychologists, and other mental health professionals in the *Diagnostic Statistical Manual, 4th Edition (DSM-IV)*, published by the American Psychiatric Association. Information about the *DSM-IV* can be found by a visit to a Web page, provided by the American Psychiatric Association, called "DSM-IV: Questions and Answers." The URL address is:

http://www.psych.org/clin_res/q_a.html

From the *American Psychiatric Association* master site it is possible to link to many mental health brochure-like articles, FAQs, various full-text scholarly documents, and many databases and archives related to psychiatry or its sub-fields (e.g., forensic psychiatry).

The *Western Psychiatric Institute and Clinic Library* is another master site for psychiatry and mental health resources. The site contains many self-help articles, links to electronic journals, research articles, and professional organizations related to psychiatry. You can find what you want quickly by using their search tool.

OPPONENT IDEAS

The Internet presents a diverse set of perspectives on mental illness and treatment. In your travels along the "information highway" you are bound to come across some sites expressing ideas that are in opposition to mainstream psychology and psychiatry. For instance, the *Center for the Study of Psychiatry and Psychology (CSPP)* site is maintained by an organization whose goal is to present opposing views about the potential dangers of drugs, electroshock therapy (ECT), psychosurgeries, and the biological theories of psychiatry. Their URL address is:

http://www.breggin.com

Another site which specializes in the controversy surrounding ECT is *Shocked: 40,000 Volts of Fun*. At this site you will find statements from the National Institute of Health (NIH) and the American Psychiatric Association about their current position on the use of electroshock therapy as a treatment for mental illness. On the other hand, there are abundant statements from ECT "survivors" and others which expose the "truth" about ECT. From this site you can link to the *Dendron* Web site, which discusses medication therapy and involuntary outpatient commitment, or the *Committee for Truth in Psychiatry* site, which uses the FAQ format to present extensive information about ECT. The *Shocked* site can be reached at the following URL address:

http://www.i1.net/~juli/shocked.html

CHAPTER 4
WEB RESOURCES ON PSYCHOLOGICAL DISORDERS

Many of the Internet sites designed for psychology consumers and mental health professionals have descriptions of psychological disorders as the bulk of their content. For those persons who are trying to understand the significance of a disorder that may have affected them or their friends or loved ones, these sites give information that may give them hope and a better understanding of symptoms, causes, and treatment options. The information is often so complete that a health practitioner can find an extensive database of information that will add to his or her professional expertise. Those who are attempting to do self-diagnosis, however, are repeatedly advised to seek professional help.

WEB DIAGNOSIS
Symptom lists based on the DSM-IV, written for an extensive variety of psychological disorders, can be found at *Mental Health Net*. Summarized versions of official diagnostic criteria for a large number of disorders, written by Dr. John Grohol, are divided into three categories: Adult, Childhood, and Personality Disorders. A short self-help questionnaire for self-diagnosis is also provided.

DATABASES ON PSYCHOLOGICAL DISORDERS
Several psychology master sites have long lists of psychological disorders arranged alphabetically or categorized by topic. These sites will give you much more than symptom lists. They will provide you with articles about the disorder, essays written by people afflicted with the disorder, research findings, and national or local organizations that you can contact to receive support services. One such site is *Mental Health.Com*. Here you will find 52 of the most common mental disorders, categorized by type of disorder. For example, there are categories for anxiety disorders and childhood disorders, and each category has several links to information related to the category. This arrangement may be helpful to the college student taking an abnormal psychology course, who will find chapter headings in the textbook that are similar to these categories. They also have a 14-page index with all the links presented at their site listed in alphabetical order. At the time of this writing, over 350,000 Internet users had visited this popular site since September, 1995.

Another master site with psychological disorders arranged by category is *Clinical Psychology Resources*. The site does not have a category devoted to childhood disorders, but there is an extensive amount of information pertaining to all the other major categories and there is a very large amount of information related to psychophysiological disorders in a section called "Behavioral Medicine."

The following is a listing in alphabetical order of very good Web pages devoted to particular disorders. This is only a sample of what is waiting for you on the WWW!

Agoraphobia and other Mental Disorders
http://www.cris.com/~danarius/mental.htm

Alzheimer Web
http://werple.mira.net.au/~dhs/ad.html

The Anxiety-Panic Internet Resource
http://www.algy.com/anxiety/anxiety.html

One A.D.D. Place: The Attention Deficit Disorder (AD/HD & LD) Community Hub
http://www.greatconnect.com/oneaddplace/

The Autism Society of America Home Page
http://www.autism-society.org/

BDP Central (about borderline personality disorder)
http://members.aol.com/BPDCentral/index.html

Bipolar Disorder Information
http://www.pendulum.org/info.htm

Brain Disorders Network
http://www.brainnet.org

Dr. Ivan's Depression Central
http://www.psycom.net/depression.central.html

Orton Dyslexia Society
http://ods.org/

Center for Eating Disorders
http://www.eating-disorders.com/

Washington University Comprehensive Epilepsy Program
http://www.neuro.wustl.edu/epilepsy

ld OnLine (about learning disabilities)
http://www.ldonline.org/

The Arc Home Page (about mental retardation)
http://thearc.org/welcome.html

Divided Hearts MPD/DID Info & Support Web (about multiple personality disorder)
http://www.dhearts.org/

Obsessive-Compulsive Disorder
http://www.fairlite.com/ocd/

Post Traumatic Stress Resources Web Page
http://www.long-beach.va.gov/ptsd/stress.html

CHAPTER 5
ASSESSMENT, TREATMENT, AND PREVENTION RESOURCES ON THE WEB

The Web offers hundreds of resources related to medical, neurological, and psychological assessment. Web resources pertaining to various forms of treatment are also plentiful. In addition, the Web will give you clinical referrals, access to online mental health services and support group discussions, and links to national or local self-help organizations.

NEUROLOGICAL ASSESSMENT
The *Neuropsychology Central* Web site provides links to a number of tests, scales, checklists and batteries related to neuropsychological assessment and also has links to several articles about this topic. The site also provides links to a number of resources related to neuropsychological treatment and rehabilitation. It is a good place to start a search for general neuroscience information on the Web.

PSYCHOLOGICAL TESTING ON THE WEB
Many of the most valid and reliable psychological tests are not available to the general public because they provide the most valuable data when they are administered and interpreted by trained professionals.. However, it is possible to find reviews/descriptions of these tests and information about test publishers on the Net.

One of the most reputable sources of information about psychological tests is the Buros Institute of Mental Measurement at the University of Nebraska, Lincoln. Their Internet site offers professional assistance to users of commercially published tests and promotes appropriate test selection and test use. Their URL address is:

http://www.unl.edu/buros

ERIC/AE Test Locator is another useful Web site provided jointly by the ERIC Clearinghouse on Assessment and Evaluation at the Catholic University of America, the Educational Testing Service (ETS), the Buros Institute, and Pro-Ed Test publishers. The *Test Locator* can be used to search the databases of these test publishers. For instance, the ETS database contains records of over 10,000 tests and research instruments. The *ERIC/AE Test Locator* is at the following URL address:

http://ericae2.educ.cua.edu/testcol.htm

Some actual psychological tests are offered on the Internet in their entirety; however, these tests typically are modified versions of a professional instrument and so are intended for personal use only. Some of the master sites with psychology tests for personal use only are *PsycSite, Cyber-Psych, PsychWeb,* and *Clinical Psychology Resources.* The last-mentioned site has two pages devoted to assessment and classification of mental disorders. There you will find links to several online personality tests, checklists and other assessment and diagnostic tools.

The American Psychological Association has published an FAQ to answer questions about psychological tests. It is located at the following URL address:

http://www.apa.org/science/testing.html

The University of Western Australia has made available three clinical instruments that can be downloaded for free: the Hamilton Depression Scale, the Positive and Negative Syndrome Scale, and the General Akathesia, Tardive Phenomena and Extrapyramidal Scale. Their URL address is:

http://www.general.uwa.edu.au/u/tlambert/MSCRU_instruments.html

Another good Web site for access to shareware is called *Shrink Tank*. This is a shareware list that contains lots of interesting questionnaires and psychological tests in the form of executable or program files for PC/MS DOS-type computers. You can download personality tests and rating scales that measure assertiveness, empathy, compulsive debtor tendencies, etc. The files are zipped (compressed) files and the program to unpack (decompress) the files is provided. You can download the programs to your own computer and then use them whenever you want to. Remember that shareware programs often have imperfections in the programming. Also, there frequently will be a request for donations. You can access this site with the following URL address:

http://www.shrinktank.com/psyfiles.htm

PsycSite has a very complete listing of Web sites that will point you to additional psychology-related freeware and shareware available on the Net.

WEB RESOURCES ABOUT PSYCHOTHERAPY

A good way to begin a search of the Internet for information about psychotherapy is to begin with an overview of contemporary therapy models. Beginning with one Web page, you can obtain information about a nice sampling of modern therapies such as Adlerian therapy, Gestalt therapy, and Client-Centered therapy, and each one comes with links to several additional Web sites. The Web page is called, *Welcome to the Theories and Approaches in Psychotherapy Page* and the URL address is:

http://www.gallaudet.edu/~11mgourn

Psych Web has many links to psychotherapy resources. There you will find an extensive listing of scholarly resources about therapy and counseling sorted by the type of therapeutical approach: 1) art, drama, and music therapies, 2) behavioral and cognitive approaches, 3) Eastern approaches, 4) other approaches to therapy, and 5) psychoanalytic. *Clinical Psychology Resources* is another master site with an even larger number of links to psychotherapy resources, organized into twelve categories of therapies. From these master sites, you will be able to link to many Web pages dedicated to a single type of therapeutical approach. The following list presents, in alphabetical order by type of therapy, a small sampling of these Web sites. A search of the Web will produce many more.

Art Therapy on the Web
http://www.sofer.com/art-therapy/

The Child and Adolescent Psychoanalysis and Psychotherapy Web Page
http://www.westnet.com/~pbrand/

Association for Death Education and Counseling
http://www.adec.org/

Department of Family Therapy: MFT Resources on the World Wide Web
http://www.nova.edu/ssss/FT/web.html

The Gestalt Therapy Page
http://www.gestalt.org/index.htm

The Liberation Psychotherapy Homepage
http:/www./liberationpsych.org/

Narrative Therapy Page
http://onthenet.com.au/~pict/mentnarr.htm

The Primal Psychotherapy Page
http://www.net-connect.net/~jspeyrer/

Albert Ellis Institute (for Rational-Emotive Therapy)
http://www.iret.org/

MEDICATIONS

Mental Health.Com is a good place to begin searching for information on medications used in the treatment of psychological disorders. This site will give you information about the "67 most common psychiatric drugs," including information about indications, contraindications, warnings, precautions, adverse effects, overdose, dosage, and research findings. The *American Psychiatric Association* Web site includes a search service, "Rx List," for a very large database of drug information on the Internet. The *National Alliance for the Mentally Ill (NAMI)* Web site, designed for people with severe mental illness and their loved ones, will enable you to access an extensive listing of links to articles about medications.

CLINICAL REFERRALS

Online Psych and *Cyber-Psych* are two master sites that have information on therapists around the country who are advertising themselves and their services. *Online Psych*'s "Treatment Locator Network" has 75,000 links to psychotherapists and other professional clinicians in the United States and around the world.. You can search the listings by geographical location to find one in your area. You can also search the listings by insurance provider, treatment modality, or population (children, adult, geriatric, etc.). In almost all cases, services are face-to-face and provided for a fee. The site also has a very good article about how to choose a therapist.

Some Web pages that are dedicated to a particular therapy will have a referral list of therapists who have had specialized training in that area. For instance, the *Albert Ellis Institute* Web page has a link to a referral list of rational-emotive behavior psychotherapists who are a Fellow or Associate Fellow of the Institute in good standing and are state-licensed. Again, their Web page can be found at the following URL address:

http://www.iret.org

More lists of service providers are likely to appear on the Internet as the medium becomes more accessible to the psychology consumer.

CLINICAL SERVICES ONLINE

NetPsych.Com is a good place to begin a look at this type of service. This Web site is dedicated to exploring the uses of the Internet to deliver mental health services. It focuses on online services such as telecounselng, newsgroups, mailing lists, and chat sessions. For instance, there is a link to *Samaritans*, a Web site in England that offers crisis counseling by E-mail and is manned by trained volunteers. Much like a crisis hot-line, their emphasis is on preventing suicide. There are other links to professionals who provide answers to questions submitted by users, much like a "Dear Abbey" service. You will even find a link to information about a commercial self-help computerized program that can be purchased for a small fee and comes with E-mail support for one year. The URL address for *NetPsych.Com* is:

http://www.netpsych.com/

NetPsych.Com has some links to current examples of using "chat" sessions to deliver psychological services. Communication can become realistic and relatively synchronous when using talk programs that actually let you go "live." These "chat" programs result in somewhat stilted conversations, however, because the information flow is reduced by a lack of verbal cues and physical gestures, and there are timing problems. Nevertheless, with these programs and your Web connection, it is possible to conduct a "talk show" or have a consultation session in real-time. Most advanced Web browsers have a version which includes the "chat" software, and most Internet service providers have the specialized software to allow you to engage in real-time conversation on the Internet. An example of a psychology-related chat room that acts as a support group meeting is the *#ABA (Lovaas) Chat Channel Home Page*. This support and information channel has discussions between parents and professionals using Applied Behavior Analysis (ABA) to teach children with autism. "Chat" software can be downloaded at the site, and since it is shareware, payment is expected. Their URL address is:

http://www.geocities.com/Heartland/Plains/1648/

From *Cyber-Psych* you can reach a large number of psychiatrists and psychotherapists offering online services. As a way to advertise services, the site has a feature called "Therapist of the Month" where one psychotherapist volunteers to provide answers to questions submitted from users. All questions and answers are archived and can be accessed easily.

Most providers charge a small fee or ask that you send payment only if you are satisfied with the results. For instance, a psychotherapist in South Africa offers *A No Obligation Dream Analysis*

Service where, through E-mail, you can send one of your dreams along with some personal information and within 48 hours you will receive an interpretation free of charge. If you are satisfied and want to continue the correspondence, he asks that you pay for future responses if they are helpful.

Users of online clinical services must be warned that professionals in the mental health fields have many legal and ethical concerns about delivery of online services. A committee of the American Psychological Association is currently writing guidelines for "media psychology." APA members are being asked to comment on the draft version of the guidelines and a final version will appear in the official APA publication, *American Psychologist*. A very good article on the ethical implications of online services by professionals has been published in the *APA Monitor* and is available online at the following URL address:

http://www.apa.org.monitor.nov95/online.html

The name "cybertherapy" has often been used to label online services delivered by mental health professionals. Most of these professionals prefer to use the word "consultation" or "advice giving" to describe their services, and do not claim to be doing therapy over the Internet. Nevertheless, there is a thin line dividing these types of services from psychotherapy. Many mental health professionals contend that an unknowing consumer might be misled even after receiving warnings and information about the distinctions between "cybertherapy" and face-to-face therapy.

ONLINE SUPPORT GROUPS

Most of the master psychology sites listed in Appendix B have links to newsgroups which are designed to be support groups. These groups are usually named *alt.support._____* , where the blank can be filled in with the names of various disorders. The groups provide an opportunity for discussion and provide emotional support for individuals affected by these disorders.

John Grohol's *Psych Central* is the best place to find a very complete listing of psychology and support groups providing services using the newsgroup format. In addition to the *alt.support* groups, many *alt.recovery* groups are listed. These newsgroups serve recovering addicts, alcoholics, gamblers, etc. The lists are updated frequently because new groups are often started and other groups become disbanded through lack of use.

From *Mental Health Net*, you can access the "Self-Help Sourcebook," which provides a search tool to find a particular support group network or organization for a variety of problems and disorders. Another way to find support groups and organizations is to go to the master sites *Mental Health.Com* or *Online Psych*. These Web sites present information about various psychological problems and disorders by category. In each category you will find links to mailing lists and *alt.support* groups pertaining to the disorders in the category.

If you would like to jump right into ongoing discussion about various topics without having to join a newsgroup, try *Mental Health Net*'s discussion forums. Using a format involving E-mail, they offer discussions on a number of mental health topics, such as friends and family or medications, and also offer a number of forums that function as support groups. In each discussion forum, you can view a history of postings and then decide if you would like to post a message to the discussion. If your Web browser supports E-mail, you can do so immediately.

PSYCHOLOGY AND THE LAW

Psych Web has a listing of resources related to forensic psychology in its "Scholarly Resources" section. This is a good place to start searching for information related to psychology and the law. The *American Psychiatric Association* site has links to the American Academy of Psychiatry and the Law and links to other forensic psychiatry sites. From these varied sources you will find many forensic psychiatry-related references, either full-text articles, abstracts, or merely references in a bibliography.

The *Bazelon Center for Mental Health Law* is a Web site dedicated to legal advocacy for the civil rights and human dignity of people with mental disabilities. Among other resources, the site includes online articles explaining key legal and policy issues in everyday terms.

WEB CONTRIBUTIONS TO PREVENTION

Several master sites in Appendix B provide the psychology consumer with a large number of self-help references. *Psych Web* has a collection of links to self-help pages on the Web sorted by topic. *Cyber-Psych* and *Mental Health Net* also have a large collection of links to self-help resources. The *NAMI* Web site provides information about their grass-roots, self-help support and advocacy organization, which has a membership that mainly consists of consumers, family memers, and friends of people who suffer from mental illness.

In addition, *Dr. Bob's Mental Health Links* is a site designed especially for the psychology student as a consumer. From this site, students can link to student counseling centers at major universities around the country. The centers often have information about problems likely to be of concern to college students, such as sexuality, relationships, alcohol, and depression. You can access this site at the following URL address:

http://uhs.bsd.uchicago.edu/~bhsiung/mental.html

An example of one of the many sources of databases on the Internet with prevention materials is the *Prevline* Web site. *Prevline*, presented by the National Clearinghouse for Drug and Alcohol Information, provides nine searchable databases with prevention material pertaining to alcohol, tobacco, marijuana, cocaine, and other drugs. The URL address for *Prevline* is:

http://www.health.org/

Another specialized free search service has been developed by the National Mental Health Services. Their *Knowledge Exchange Network (KEN)* is designed to be a one-stop source. You can currently search the Web pages of 1,800 private organizations and government agencies that provide mental health services and information. *KEN* has recently added two new searchable databases to their Web site: the Consumer/Survivor Database and the 1995 Mental Health Directory. Their URL address is:

http://www.mentalhealth.org

With the capability of the Internet to reach thousands of users, this medium is a valuable tool for spreading information about a subject that is poorly understood. For many years, the U.S. has carried out a media campaign to bring information about psychological disorders to the public in a variety of media messages, in the hope that some forms of mental illness could be prevented, or at least, not worsened. A secondary goal has been an effort to reduce the stigma of mental illness that comes with misunderstanding. All of the master sites listed in Appendix B have made valuable and substantial contributions to the prevention movement by making information about mental health and mental illness available to the general public in formats that are easy to understand. These sites are accessed by thousands of individuals each day who find hope in their quest to understand the problems in their lives and find support and services to help alleviate their distress.

CHAPTER 6
WEB RESOURCES FOR CONTINUING EDUCATION IN ABNORMAL PSYCHOLOGY

Membership in professional organizations has always been a major resource for continuing education. These organizations typically provide conference, seminar, and workshop information. The organizations' newsletters and magazines typically provide job listings and updates on current events and hot issues in the field. Now you can get all of the above and more on the Internet by simply accessing the home pages of these organizations and going from there. Several other sites also provide resources for continuing education.

PROFESSIONAL ORGANIZATIONS AND SOCIETIES
From the home page of any major psychology organization, you can fill out a membership application form online and then mail, E-mail, or fax it; but even without membership status, you can browse the pages of the organization and gain access to abundant information.

The home pages usually give conference information, continuing education opportunities, job listings, and more. Most will have links to major psychology resource listings. Sites such as the American Psychological Association's *PsychNET* or the *American Psychiatric Association* home page are great starting places for finding continuing education resources on the Internet. Most of the master sites listed in Appendix B have a large number of links to a variety of psychology organizations and societies. You can see such a list by accessing *PsycSite*.

CONFERENCES, WORKSHOPS, AND SEMINARS
All of the professional organizations and societies will have lists of their own conferences and maybe some links to other education resources. Some commercial sites, acting as information services, will give much more extensive listings. *Online Psych* lists conferences, seminars, and workshops related to clinical and counseling psychology. *Mental Health Infosource* is a Web site provided by CME, Inc. which provides continuing medical education for psychiatrists. There are listings of many audio and video courses for home study, listings of associations and meetings (with online registration), and resources related to the latest information about psychiatric medications.

PsychScapes WorldWide, Inc. Web site has a very extensive and continually updated list that includes many conferences, workshops, and seminars for mental health professionals, and also includes personal growth workshops that are of more general interest. Their URL address is:

http://www.mental-health.com/PsychScapes/home.html

The *National Institute of Mental Health (NIMH)* "Calendar of Events" also provides a good list of conferences and other events related to psychology. In addition, the *NIMH* site will give you information on research fellowships and grants funded by the National Institute of Health (NIH) and other related organizations. The *NIMH* home page is located at the following URL address:

http://www.nimh.nih.gov/

JOB LISTINGS

Of course, the American Psychological Association and the American Psychiatric Association are two very good sources of mental health job openings. *PsycSite* and *Psych Web* also provide links to employment information sources.

Job openings at the NIH and fellowship opportunities are listed at the *NIMH* site.

NEWS UPDATES AND CURRENT EVENTS

A good way to keep up with news in the field of psychology and current events affecting the field is to browse the publications from the Web sites of the major professional organizations. The *American Psychiatric Association* site contains articles from the *Psychiatric News*, and *PsychNET* contains selections from the *APA Monitor.*

The *Mental Health Infosource* site contains press releases on topics related to the latest developments in mental illness and mental health, and publishes several full-text articles from *Psychiatric Times.* The articles are arranged by topic to make it is easier to find what you are looking for. The site also contains regular columns by professionals who provide commentaries on popular issues in the mental health field.

The *NAMI* Web site, dedicated to reducing the stigma of and ignorance about mental illness, provides a "press room" loaded with updates on legislation and policy issues related to mental illness, and a very large number of links to information about the latest research findings.

APPENDIX A
GLOSSARY OF TERMS

bookmark   A function of the Internet browser that lets you set a placeholder for a particular Web address so that you can return to it easily.

browser   Software that lets you view Web pages.

client   According to the client-server model, software that requests services from another computer (server).

download   Using a browser or FTP program, getting software to your computer from another.

FAQ   Frequently Asked Questions is a document that covers basic information about a topic or discussion group in a question-and-answer format.

FTP   File Transfer Protocol is software for moving files from one computer to another.   Some FTP servers allow public log-on by *Anonymous FTP* procedures.

Gopher   A program that provides access to organized Internet resources by having the user move through hierarchical menus.

HTML   Hypertext Markup Language used to write documents that appear on the Web, specifying format, graphics, and links to other documents.

HTTP   HyperText Transfer Protocol for information transmission between computers that use the World Wide Web.

LISTSERV   A program that manages electronic mailing lists and their distribution functions.

newsgroup   The name used to describe a topical discussion group that is part of a world-wide network, USENET.

server   According to the client-server model, software that answers requests from a client program.

URL   Uniform Resources Locator standard format for indicating addresses of Internet sites by describing information transmission protocol, the exact location of the file, and the file name.

USENET   A world-wide network of newsgroups using NNTP protocol for the exchange of messages over the Internet. An Internet service provider must have a USENET server to provide this service to its client customers.

WAIS   Wide Area Information Server that allows you to search databases by keyword.

APPENDIX B
MASTER SITES RELATED TO ABNORMAL PSYCHOLOGY

The pages in this appendix describe a set of Web sites (on the Internet at the time of this writing) that we call "master sites" because they contain a tremendous amount of information regarding resources related to abnormal psychology. The site descriptions are presented in alphabetical order.

For each site, the resources are listed in tabular form and divided into four parts. The first part of the table lets you know if general mental health information intended for the general public is available at the site. The second part describes what scholarly information is available at the site. The third part lets you know if the site has links to various support services, and the last part of the table lets you know if the site contains resources related to continuing education and training in psychology and psychiatry. Hopefully, these site descriptions will give you a quick overview of what each master site contains and will make it easier for you to get to the information you want.

Most of these sites are provided by reputable professional organizations, educational institutions, and commercial enterprises. Nevertheless, users are warned that no attempt has been made to evaluate the resources, and the authors cannot take responsibility for the accuracy of information at any site.

If you go to one of these sites and it suits your needs, we suggest that you bookmark it using your Web browser.

HOME PAGE: **American Psychiatric Association**

URL ADDRESS: **http://www.psych.org**

RESOURCES

Mental Health References
- __x_ Self-help articles/brochures
- __x_ FAQs
- ____ Diagnostic criteria/tests
- __x_ News updates/current events

Research References
- __x_ Research articles/abstracts
- __x_ Research institutes/centers
- __x_ Databases/archives/bibliographies
- __x_ Resources organized by topic
- __x_ Search tools
- __x_ Lists of books/magazines/journals
- ____ Bookstores/publishers

Support Services
- __x_ Shareware/commercial software
- ____ Clinical referrals/treatment locator
- ____ On-line clinical/counseling services
- __x_ Newsgroups/discussions/mailing lists
- __x_ Support organizations
- ____ Chat room

Continuing Education
- __x_ Professional organizations/societies/conferences
- __x_ Professional seminars/training/continuing education
- ____ Graduate schools/universities/departments

DESCRIPTION: This is the site of the national organization for psychiatrists. There is a limited amount of self-help information for the psychology consumer. Most of the resources are designed for professionals who want to get continuing education or read news about recent legislation and other current issues in the field. There are some good links to forensic psychiatry sites and a search service using "RxList," a large Internet drug index.

HOME PAGE: **American Psychological Association (PsychNET)**

URL ADDRESS: **http://www.apa.org/sitemap.html**

RESOURCES

Mental Health References
- __x_ Self-help articles/brochures
- __x_ FAQs
- _____ Diagnostic criteria/tests
- __x_ News updates/current events

Research References
- __x_ Research articles/abstracts
- _____ Research institutes/centers
- __x_ Databases/archives/bibliographies
- _____ Resources organized by topic
- __x_ Search tools
- __x_ Lists of books/magazines/journals
- __x_ Bookstores/publishers

Support Services
- _____ Shareware/commercial software
- __x_ Clinical referrals/treatment locator
- _____ On-line clinical/counseling services
- __x_ Newsgroups/discussions/mailing lists
- _____ Support organizations
- _____ Chat room

Continuing Education
- __x_ Professional organizations/societies/conferences
- __x_ Professional seminars/training/continuing education
- __x_ Graduate schools/universities/departments

DESCRIPTION: This home page for the American Psychological Association presents information for the general public about psychology and is a major resource for the professional psychologist. Media releases, mental health brochures, and selected articles from the *APA Monitor* are some of its features. *PsychCrawler*, located at the site, is a new search engine that will search the indices of the APA and National Institute of Mental Health (NIMH) Web sites.

HOME PAGE: **Clinical Psychology Resources**

URL ADDRESS: **http://www.psychologie.uni-bonn.de/kap/li_home.htm**

RESOURCES

Mental Health References
- __x_ Self-help articles/brochures
- __x_ FAQs
- __x_ Diagnostic criteria/tests
- ____ News updates/current events

Research References
- __x_ Research articles/abstracts
- __x_ Research institutes/centers
- __x_ Databases/archives/bibliographies
- __x_ Resources organized by topic
- __x_ Search tools
- __x_ Lists of books/magazines/journals
- __x_ Bookstores/publishers

Support Services
- __x_ Shareware/commercial software
- ____ Clinical referrals/treatment locator
- __x_ On-line clinical/counseling services
- ____ Newsgroups/discussions/mailing lists
- __x_ Support organizations
- ____ Chat room

Continuing Education
- ____ Professional organizations/societies/conferences
- ____ Professional seminars/training/continuing education
- __x_ Graduate schools/universities/departments

DESCRIPTION: Clinical Psychology Resources is an outstanding German master site for clinical and abnormal psychology, behavioral medicine, and mental health. The site contains information pertaining to a number of disorders (organized by type of disorder) and covers a wide variety of clinical issues pertaining to assessment and psychotherapy. There are also a great number of links to psychological online documents, though these are not categorized.

HOME PAGE: **Cyber-Psych**

URL ADDRESS: **http://www.webweaver.net/psych**

RESOURCES

Mental Health References
- __x_ Self-help articles/brochures
- __x_ FAQs
- __x_ Diagnostic criteria/tests
- ____ News updates/current events

Research References
- ____ Research articles/abstracts
- __x_ Research institutes/centers
- __x_ Databases/archives/bibliographies
- __x_ Resources organized by topic
- ____ Search tools
- __x_ Lists of books/magazines/journals
- ____ Bookstores/publishers

Support Services
- ____ Shareware/commercial software
- __x_ Clinical referrals/treatment locator
- __x_ On-line clinical/counseling services
- __x_ Newsgroups/discussions/mailing lists
- __x_ Support organizations
- ____ Chat room

Continuing Education
- __x_ Professional organizations/societies/conferences
- ____ Professional seminars/training/continuing education
- __x_ Graduate schools/universities/departments

DESCRIPTION: This is a master site that lists online resources for a limited number of mental health issues. Cyber-Psych describes itself as a service bringing professional psychological care and information to the online community in a non-threatening, interactive format.

HOME PAGE: **Mental Health.Com**

URL ADDRESS: **http://www.mentalhealth.com/main.html**

RESOURCES

Mental Health References
- _x_   Self-help articles/brochures
- _x_   FAQs
- _x_   Diagnostic criteria/tests
- _x_   News updates/current events

Research References
- _x_   Research articles/abstracts
- _x_   Research institutes/centers
- _x_   Databases/archives/bibliographies
- _x_   Resources organized by topic
- _x_   Search tools
- _x_   Lists of books/magazines/journals
- ___   Bookstores/publishers

Support Services
- ___   Shareware/commercial software
- ___   Clinical referrals/treatment locator
- _x_   On-line clinical/counseling services
- _x_   Newsgroups/discussions/mailing lists
- _x_   Support organizations
- ___   Chat room

Continuing Education
- _x_   Professional organizations/societies/conferences
- ___   Professional seminars/training/continuing education
- _x_   Graduate schools/universities/departments

DESCRIPTION: MentalHealth.Com is a master site for mental health information. There is lots of self-help information in the form of fact sheets and FAQs, and there are many links to research databases. They describe themselves as a site designed to share mental health information with the world. Resources pertaining to diagnosis and treatment of mental illness are listed categorically by disorder.

HOME PAGE: **Mental Health Infosource**

URL ADDRESS: **http://www.mhsource.com/**

RESOURCES

Mental Health References
_x_ Self-help articles/brochures
___ FAQs
_x_ Diagnostic criteria/tests
_x_ News updates/current events

Research References
_x_ Research articles/abstracts
___ Research institutes/centers
___ Databases/archives/bibliographies
_x_ Resources organized by topic
_x_ Search tools
___ Lists of books/magazines/journals
___ Bookstores/publishers

Support Services
___ Shareware/commercial software
___ Clinical referrals/treatment locator
_x_ On-line clinical/counseling services
_x_ Newsgroups/discussions/mailing lists
___ Support organizations
_x_ Chat room

Continuing Education
___ Professional organizations/societies/conferences
_x_ Professional seminars/training/continuing education
___ Graduate schools/universities/departments

DESCRIPTION: This Web site is provided by CME, Inc., which provides continuing medical education credit for physicians, and so the site has several resources for the mental health professional. The psychology consumer will also find the site interesting because it offers interesting reading on current events and current ideas in the field of psychiatry. Complete articles from *Psychiatric Times* and commentaries by professional columnists are published online. There is also an "Ask the Expert" column which goes live in a "chat room" format occasionally, and there are other chat rooms for advocates, patients, and family members to discuss relevant issues.

HOME PAGE: **Mental Health Net**

URL ADDRESS: **http://www.cmhc.com**

RESOURCES

Mental Health References
_x_   Self-help articles/brochures
_x_   FAQs
_x_   Diagnostic criteria/tests
_x_   News updates/current events

Research References
____   Research articles/abstracts
____   Research institutes/centers
_x_   Databases/archives/bibliographies
_x_   Resources organized by topic
_x_   Search tools
_x_   Lists of books/magazines/journals
____   Bookstores/publishers

Support Services
_x_   Shareware/commercial software
_x_   Clinical referrals/treatment locator
_x_   On-line clinical/counseling services
_x_   Newsgroups/discussions/mailing lists
_x_   Support organizations
____   Chat room

Continuing Education
____   Professional organizations/societies/conferences
____   Professional seminars/training/continuing education
____   Graduate schools/universities/departments

DESCRIPTION: Mental Health Net is a master site for mental health information. The site claims to feature over 6,000 links, and provides professional and self-help information on a wide variety of disorders. Information about diagnosis and treatment options is arranged in categories according to disorder. The "Self-Help Sourcebook Online" is a useful search tool for finding out about organizations or newsgroups dedicated to self-help and support. Another unique feature is the large number of discussion forums on various disorders, general issues, or more specific topics such as "medication."

HOME PAGE: **National Alliance for the Mentally Ill (NAMI)**

URL ADDRESS: **http://www.nami.org/index.html**

RESOURCES

Mental Health References
_x_ Self-help articles/brochures
___ FAQs
___ Diagnostic criteria/tests
_x_ News updates/current events

Research References
_x_ Research articles/abstracts
___ Research institutes/centers
___ Databases/archives/bibliographies
___ Resources organized by topic
_x_ Search tools
_x_ Lists of books/magazines/journals
___ Bookstores/publishers

Support Services
___ Shareware/commercial software
___ Clinical referrals/treatment locator
___ On-line clinical/counseling services
___ Newsgroups/discussions/mailing lists
_x_ Support organizations
___ Chat room

Continuing Education
_x_ Professional organizations/societies/conferences
___ Professional seminars/training/continuing education
___ Graduate schools/universities/departments

DESCRIPTION: The NAMI site is an advocacy and self-help organization dedicated to improving the lives of people with mental illness, their families, friends, and loved ones. Much of the site contains press updates, recent research results, and information on recent legislation in this area. The site has many links to mental health fact sheets and support organizations, and there are several resources related to medications. Their purpose is to educate the general public about mental illness and reduce some of the stigma attached to it.

HOME PAGE: **Neuropsychology Central**

URL ADDRESS: **http://www.premier.net/~cogito/neuropsy.html**

RESOURCES

Mental Health References
__x_ Self-help articles/brochures
__x_ FAQs
__x_ Diagnostic criteria/tests
____ News updates/current events

Research References
__x_ Research articles/abstracts
__x_ Research institutes/centers
__x_ Databases/archives/bibliographies
__x_ Resources organized by topic
__x_ Search tools
____ Lists of books/magazines/journals
____ Bookstores/publishers

Support Services
__x_ Shareware/commercial software
____ Clinical referrals/treatment locator
____ On-line clinical/counseling services
__x_ Newsgroups/discussions/mailing lists
____ Support organizations
____ Chat room

Continuing Education
__x_ Professional organizations/societies/conferences
__x_ Professional seminars/training/continuing education
__x_ Graduate schools/universities/departments

DESCRIPTION: The site is a very comprehensive set of resources pertaining to the understanding, diagnosis, and treatment of neuropsychological disorders. Developmental and geriatric resources are included. Resources pertaining to treatment of neuropsychological disorders are categorized by disorder. Professionals will find helpful full-text research articles from major neuropsychology laboratories in the U.S. and abroad, and can participate in discussion forums. The psychology consumer will find self-help fact sheets and support organizations. There is something for everyone.

HOME PAGE: **Online Psych**

URL ADDRESS: **http://www.onlinepsych.com**

RESOURCES

Mental Health References
_x_ Self-help articles/brochures
_x_ FAQs
___ Diagnostic criteria/tests
___ News updates/current events

Research References
___ Research articles/abstracts
_x_ Research institutes/centers
_x_ Databases/archives/bibliographies
_x_ Resources organized by topic
_x_ Search tools
_x_ Lists of books/magazines/journals
_x_ Bookstores/publishers

Support Services
___ Shareware/commercial software
___ Clinical referrals/treatment locator
_x_ On-line clinical/counseling services
_x_ Newsgroups/discussions/mailing lists
_x_ Support organizations
___ Chat room

Continuing Education
___ Professional organizations/societies/conferences
_x_ Professional seminars/training/continuing education
___ Graduate schools/universities/departments

DESCRIPTION: Online Psych describes itself as a comprehensive information service. Information about disorders and treatment options is organized into over 25 topical areas arranged alphabetically. The site offers a mental health treatment locator service with 75,000 listings in the U.S. and abroad.

HOME PAGE: **Psych Central**

URL ADDRESS: **http://www.coil.com/~grohol**

RESOURCES

Mental Health References
__x_ Self-help articles/brochures
__x_ FAQs
__x_ Diagnostic criteria/tests
____ News updates/current events

Research References
____ Research articles/abstracts
____ Research institutes/centers
____ Databases/archives/bibliographies
____ Resources organized by topic
____ Search tools
__x_ Lists of books/magazines/journals
____ Bookstores/publishers

Support Services
____ Shareware/commercial software
____ Clinical referrals/treatment locator
__x_ On-line clinical/counseling services
__x_ Newsgroups/discussions/mailing lists
__x_ Support organizations
__x_ Chat room

Continuing Education
__x_ Professional organizations/societies/conferences
____ Professional seminars/training/continuing education
__x_ Graduate schools/universities/departments

DESCRIPTION: Psych Central is a master site also known as Dr. John Grohol's Mental Health Page. Psych Central provides a comprehensive list of Internet links to mental health issues, psychology, and support resources. The site contains a very complete list of pointers to psychology-related mailing lists and newsgroups.

HOME PAGE: **Psych Web**

URL ADDRESS: **http://www.gasou.edu/psychweb/psychweb.htm**

RESOURCES

Mental Health References
__x_ Self-help articles/brochures
__x_ FAQs
__x_ Diagnostic criteria/tests
_____ News updates/current events

Research References
_____ Research articles/abstracts
__x_ Research institutes/centers
__x_ Databases/archives/bibliographies
__x_ Resources organized by topic
_____ Search tools
__x_ Lists of books/magazines/journals
_____ Bookstores/publishers

Support Services
__x_ Shareware/commercial software
_____ Clinical referrals/treatment locator
_____ On-line clinical/counseling services
__x_ Newsgroups/discussions/mailing lists
__x_ Support organizations
_____ Chat room

Continuing Education
__x_ Professional organizations/societies/conferences
_____ Professional seminars/training/continuing education
__x_ Graduate schools/universities/departments

DESCRIPTION: Psych Web is a master site for psychology related information. It describes itself as a site for students and teachers of psychology. The site is comprehensive, with listings of resources divided into self-help and scholarly categories, but the organization is not as good as it could be. It is especially suited for psychology students, with many "tip sheets" related to psychology careers, graduate study, and other issues of concern to students.

HOME PAGE: **PsycSite**

URL ADDRESS: **http://www.unipissing.ca/psyc/psycsite.htm**

RESOURCES

Mental Health References

_____ Self-help articles/brochures
_____ FAQs
_____ Diagnostic criteria/tests
_____ News updates/current events

Research References

__x_ Research articles/abstracts
_____ Research institutes/centers
__x_ Databases/archives/bibliographies
__x_ Resources organized by topic
__x_ Search tools
__x_ Lists of books/magazines/journals
_____ Bookstores/publishers

Support Services

__x_ Shareware/commercial software
_____ Clinical referrals/treatment locator
__x_ On-line clinical/counseling services
__x_ Newsgroups/discussions/mailing lists
_____ Support organizations
__x_ Chat room

Continuing Education

__x_ Professional organizations/societies/conferences
_____ Professional seminars/training/continuing education
__x_ Graduate schools/universities/departments

DESCRIPTION: PsycSite, brought to you from Canada, is one of the best master sites available for resources that focus on the science of psychology. PsycSite describes itself as a "launch pad" to Net sites of interest to psychologists, students, and others interested in psychological science. Internet sites that deal with self-help or parapsychology are excluded from the listings at this site. There are a very large number of pointers to journals, abstracts, and databases, and they are organized by topic. Some links lead to full-text scholarly articles published online.

HOME PAGE: **Western Psiychiatric Institute and Clinic Library**

URL ADDRESS: **http://www.wpic.library.pitt.edu**

RESOURCES

Mental Health References

__x_ Self-help articles/brochures
____ FAQs
__x_ Diagnostic criteria/tests
__x_ News updates/current events

Research References

__x_ Research articles/abstracts
__x_ Research institutes/centers
__x_ Databases/archives/bibliographies
__x_ Resources organized by topic
__x_ Search tools
__x_ Lists of books/magazines/journals
__x_ Bookstores/publishers

Support Services

__x_ Shareware/commercial software
____ Clinical referrals/treatment locator
____ On-line clinical/counseling services
__x_ Newsgroups/discussions/mailing lists
____ Support organizations
__x_ Chat room

Continuing Education

__x_ Professional organizations/societies/conferences
__x_ Professional seminars/training/continuing education
__x_ Graduate schools/universities/departments

DESCRIPTION: This site carries much information related to psychiatry and mental health and is designed for professionals and consumers. The library has every kind of resource available, including research articles, databases, and a good list of electronic mental health journals and newspapers. For the consumer, there are self-help articles and a special feature called "Consumer Chat," which is a scheduled online chat session for advocates, patients, and their families to discuss mental health issues.